isbn# 0-7948-0719-4

H.E. Harris & Co. ®
Serving the Collector Since 1916

10   9   8   7   6   5   4   3   2   1

FIRST PRINTING

THE OFFICIAL U.S. MINT

STORIES OF THE
2000

50
STATE
QUARTERS

TM

© 1998 U.S.MINT

H.E. Harris & Co.®
Serving the Collector Since 1916

PROGRAM

If you flip over any of the 50 State Quarters™ Program coins, you will see that each has a different state design on its tail side (known as the reverse). In 1997, Congress passed an Act that established the 50 State Quarters™ Program. The program calls for the production of five new quarters every year for ten years. These commemorative quarters honor each state by featuring a symbol of its history, and are issued in the order that the state accepted the U.S. Constitution and entered the Union.

The many changes in the quarter's design are historical firsts, and are especially noteworthy considering how little the quarter has changed since its birth. The first quarter was minted in 1796, and was originally made of silver. The Mint Act of April 2, 1792, called for the quarter design to feature the date the quarter was minted, the word "Liberty," and an image representing liberty. The image chosen was Lady Liberty, a woman in long robes with gently flowing hair. For over 115 years, she represented the idea of liberty on the quarter's front (called the obverse). Although the style of Lady Liberty's dress and hair changed over the years, it was not until George Washington's 200th birthday in 1932 that the first president replaced Liberty on the obverse of the 25 cent coin.

From the beginning of the 50 State Quarters™ Program in 1999, through its end in 2008, the reverse of the coin will change 50 times. Each coin will not only represent a part of our nation's remarkable past, but will also be a piece of history itself.

UNITED STATES

LIBERTY

QUARTER DO

Capital: Boston

State Flower: Mayflower

State Tree: American Elm

State Bird: Chickadee

Land Area: 7,838 sq. mi.

Rank in Size (Land Area): 45th

State Song: "All Hail to Massachusetts"

Largest City: Boston

Statehood Date: February 6, 1788

Nickname: Bay State

The bravery and commitment of the minutemen was honored on the Massachusetts quarter.

Massachusetts was named after a local tribe whose name means "at or about the great hill."

MASSACHUSETTS: BY THE SWORD WE SEEK PEACE, BUT PEACE ONLY UNDER LIBERTY

When the Pilgrims first stepped from the Mayflower onto Plymouth Rock in 1620, there were already many Native American tribes that called the Massachusetts area their home. Among these were the Pennacook, Nauset, Wampanoag, and Massachuset tribes. Massachusetts received its name from Captain John Smith of Virginia, after meeting the Massachuset tribe while exploring the land in 1614. (Massachuset is actually a Native American word for "Great Hill," believed to refer to the tallest of the Blue Hills just outside of Milton.) In fact, it was Smith's glowing words about the area's beauty and fertility that led the Pilgrims – a religious group persecuted for their refusal to join the Church of England – to seek refuge in the New World.

By 1630, Puritans began to leave England to settle in the area, which had now been chartered as the Massachusetts Bay Colony. The Puritans laid out towns in Salem and Boston, where they established a system of government, and the practice of town meetings, that would later contribute to the style of government we have today. It was these Puritan and Pilgrim settlements along Massachusetts's many bays that later earned the state the nicknames "The Bay State" and "The Old Bay State."

In more recent times, people often refer to this section of New England as "The Bean State." In the colonial period, sugar cane was sent to Boston to be made into rum and exported, but some was reserved for molasses used to slow-bake beans. The capital, Boston, is lovingly called "Bean Town."

IN A MASSACHUSETTS MINUTE

The rugged-looking man featured on the reverse, or back, of the Massachusetts quarter is based on a statue, "The Minuteman," that stands in The Minuteman National Historical Park in Concord. The Minuteman on the quarter represents Massachusetts's tremendous contribution to our nation's freedom.

When delegates from the 13 colonies met at the Second Continental Congress in 1775, their formal declaration of independence from, and war against, England was a true act of bravery. As England had one of the most powerful militaries in the world at the time, the colonists' decision to fight in the Revolutionary War was as if a mouse had chosen to fight a lion. Britain outnumbered America with both soldiers and guns.

The patriots, however, were a clever bunch. They reorganized their militia in order to eliminate any Loyalists (those loyal to the English) from their ranks. The reformed militia contained patriotic farmers and townspeople, known as minutemen because they could be ready for action on a minute's notice. These small bands of armed men used fighting tactics that were unheard of at the time – they attacked British troops from the rear, ambushed them in towns and forests, and even disguised themselves as British soldiers.

Many minutemen were from Massachusetts. In fact, three Massachusetts minutemen, Samuel Prescott, William Dawes, and Paul Revere, took part in the famous midnight ride of April 18, 1775, that marked the beginning of the Revolutionary War. The minutemen's inventiveness, courage, and passion helped America win the war. The minuteman concept for the quarter was submitted by schoolchildren of Massachusetts.

ALLEYOOP!

The heart-pounding, gravity-defying game we all know as basketball was first played in Massachusetts. Basketball was invented on December 1, 1891, by Joseph Naismith, a physical education instructor at the YMCA training school in Springfield. Naismith set up two large peach baskets (hence the name basketball) on both ends of a court, and gave his students a list of rules that were pretty much the same as they are today. The players loved the game so much that the rules were published in their school paper. More people started playing and the rest is history.

THE AFRICAN MEETING HOUSE

Before 1805, blacks in Boston worshipped in white churches, but they were denied voting rights and were only allowed to sit in the balconies. A New Hampshire preacher named Thomas Paul began holding separate worship meetings for African Americans at Faneuil Hall in Boston. On August 8, 1805, he and twenty of his members formed the First African Baptist Church.

By 1806, Paul had raised enough money to build the first church for African Americans. The African Meeting House was established on Smith Street that year. In 1832, William Lloyd Garrison founded the New England Anti-Slavery Society at this location.

THE TRUTH ABOUT THANKSGIVING

Don't you just love Thanksgiving dinner – turkey, mashed potatoes, stuffing, candied yams, and of course, pumpkin pie? Well, the feast the Pilgrims shared with their Wampanoag neighbors in 1621 did not have quite the same menu. Although turkey was eaten at the first Thanksgiving, there was certainly no pumpkin pie – the Pilgrims' sugar supply was running awfully low in 1621. And don't tell your mom, but the Pilgrims probably did not eat their veggies at the first Thanksgiving table, since at that time feasts were mainly meat-fests.

Although today's Thanksgiving menu is different from the original, the spirit of the feast remains the same – a time to enjoy the harvest with family and friends. So pick up your fork and dig in (by the way, the Pilgrims ate with spoons and, ahem, their fingers, since the fork did not appear in America until 1630)!

DOCTOR'S ORDERS

In the city of Boston, it is illegal to take a bath unless your doctor has told you to do so.

Maryland's quarter pictures the historic dome of the State Capitol Building in Annapolis.

Capital: Annapolis

State Flower: Black-Eyed Susan

State Tree: White Oak

State Bird: Baltimore Oriole

Land Area: 9,775 sq. mi.

Rank in Size (Land Area): 42nd

State Song: "Maryland, My Maryland"

Largest City: Baltimore

Statehood Date: April 28, 1788

Nickname: Old Line State

Maryland was named to honor Queen Henrietta Maria, wife of England's King Charles I.

MARYLAND: MANLY DEEDS, WOMANLY WORDS

Maryland was established in 1633 by the Calvert family of England. The Calverts were Roman Catholic, which was frowned upon in 17th century England, where the official religion was Protestantism. Seeking a place where they and other religious people would be free to practice their faith, the Calverts came to America in 1634 and settled in a town they called St. Mary's City. They named their new colony Maryland, after the English Queen Henrietta Maria, who was also Catholic. Because Marylanders believed so strongly in religious freedom, they eventually passed the Tolerance Act in 1649, which stated that Christians of all denominations would be welcome within the colony's borders.

Maryland has had a long history of standing up for what it believes in. During the American Revolution, when colonists struggled for independence from English rule, Maryland contributed 23,000 troops to the war effort. Although no battles were fought on Maryland's soil, her men fought so bravely that General George Washington praised them as the "troops of the line" – Maryland has been called "The Old Line State" ever since.

THIS OLD STATE HOUSE

On the back of Maryland's quarter is the top of the Maryland State House, a historic landmark, surrounded by clusters of leaves from Maryland's state tree, the white oak, and flanked by the words "The Old Line State," the state's nickname.

Built in 1772, the Maryland State House stands in State Circle in Annapolis, where two previous state houses once stood. It is believed that the architect, Joseph Clark, based his design on a palace tower in Germany called the Schlossturm. Interestingly, the word "statehouse" comes from the German word "stadthaus," meaning "city hall," and the Maryland General Assembly actually called the structure the Stadt House for some time.

The State House's enormous dome is made entirely of wood, and is even held together by wooden pegs. Many historic moments have occurred beneath this wooden cupola (or dome). From November 1783 to June 1784, Annapolis served as our nation's capital. On April 11, 1783, the Continental Congress gathered in the glorious State House to declare an end to the Revolutionary War. On December 2, 1783, it was at the Maryland State House that General George Washington resigned as Commander-in-Chief of the Continental Army. And just three weeks later, in the same Old Senate

Chamber, Congress signed the Treaty of Paris, which officially ended the Revolutionary War.

Some historians say that the dome, which in traditional architecture stands for unity, strength, and permanence, represents the ideals of our Founding Fathers. The shiny, golden acorn that rests at its top is a symbol that the building, and the state and country it represents, are "sound as an acorn," or perfect and solid. Even the State House lightning rod, which was based on a design by Benjamin Franklin, is an emblem of America's independence. The Maryland State House is the oldest statehouse still in operation, and symbolizes our nation's quest for freedom.

THE NORTH POLE OR BUST!

One of the first explorers of the North Pole was Matthew Alexander Henson, an African American born in Maryland in 1866. Orphaned when very young, Henson joined the crew of the sailing ship *Katie Hines* at the ripe old age of 12, and later worked in Washington, D.C., where he met explorer Robert Peary. Peary admired Henson's intelligence and resourcefulness, and in 1888 invited him to be his assistant on an expedition to Nicaragua. Before long, he asked Henson to join him on a series of missions to explore the North Pole. In 1909, Henson was one of 6 people to make it to the North Pole, and received a Congressional medal in 1944 for his amazing achievement.

OH, SAY CAN YOU SEE?

"The Star Spangled Banner" was written during the War of 1812 by Maryland native Francis Scott Key. In 1814, the British had just burned down Washington, and Key was sent to rescue a friend who had been captured by a British fleet in the Chesapeake Bay. But when Key got there he was held aboard a ship and watched helplessly as the British shelled Fort McHenry. That night, Key barely slept. When morning came on September 14, he was so relieved to see the American flag still waving over the fort that he sat down and wrote the poem that later became our national anthem.

EARTH ANGEL

Clara Barton was an extraordinary nurse. While aiding injured soldiers during the Civil War (1861-1865), Barton was inspired to organize an agency to provide relief supplies for the wounded. By 1865, President Abraham Lincoln asked her to establish a record bureau to keep track of missing men. Even during a vacation in Europe, Barton assisted war victims at the outbreak of the Franco-German War (1870-1871). While in Europe, Barton met representatives from the International Red Cross, and was so inspired by their organization that she founded the American National Red Cross in 1881. Barton eventually expanded the Red Cross to assist not only victims of war, but also victims of natural disasters such as floods, tornadoes, and earth-quakes. Clara Barton's tireless work to help others earned her the nickname "Angel of the Battlefield."

THAT SINK STINKS!

In Baltimore, it is illegal to clean a sink, no matter how food-caked, slimy, or stinky it gets!

Capital: Columbia

State Flower: Carolina Jessamine

State Tree: Palmetto

State Bird: Carolina Wren

Land Area: 30,111 sq. mi.

Rank in Size (Land Area): 40th

State Song: "Carolina"

Largest City: Columbia

Statehood Date: May 23, 1788

Nickname: Palmetto State

The state emblems of South Carolina are featured on the reverse.

South Carolina shares the history of its name with North Carolina, named for King Charles I of England.

SOUTH CAROLINA: WHILE I BREATHE I HOPE

Before the English settled South Carolina in the 17th century, it was inhabited by the Yamasee Indians, as well as the French and Spanish. The land was claimed by the English in 1629 and named *Carolana* (meaning "land of Charles" in Latin) after King Charles I. King Charles II changed the spelling to Carolina in 1663, and the colony was eventually divided into north and south.

As with most states, South Carolina has a bunch of nicknames. One, "The Palmetto State," dates back to the American Revolution, when colonists defended themselves against a British attack by building a fort made out of palmetto logs. The tree has come to stand for South Carolina's strength.

The state contains a variety of natural environments – the warm semi-tropical islands, the marshy coastal plains, the green and hilly Piedmont region, and the Blue Ridge section of the Appalachian Mountains. South Carolina's many habitats and natural resources have earned it such nicknames as "Swamp State" for its unusual black water swamps, "Rice State" for the grain that grows so well in its warm, wet areas, and "Iodine State" for the iodine levels in the state's seaside plants.

But it may be South Carolina's nickname as "The Keystone of the South Atlantic Seaboard" that is most fitting, since the state has played such a central role in the history of the South.

PRAISE THE PALMETTO

The lovely scene on the back of South Carolina's quarter is actually made up of some of the eighth state's most treasured symbols. Against the backdrop of the state's outline is a Carolina wren, the state bird, perched on a sprig of yellow jessamine, the state flower. Below the words "The Palmetto State," is a star, representing the capital, Columbia, and just to its right is a grand palmetto tree. When choosing these objects for the quarter's design, Governor Jim Hodges explained that the song of the Carolina wren symbolizes the hospitality of South Carolina's people, the dainty springtime flower of the yellow jessamine stands for the state's natural beauty, and the palmetto represents South Carolina's enduring strength.

This palmetto tree occupies an important place in South Carolina's history. During the Revolutionary War, England made plans to attack the city of Charleston, a major Southern port town. By February 1776, Charlestonians were warned of this plan, and realized that in order to defend themselves they would have to build a fort, and build it fast. In March, Colonel William Moultrie chose a spot for the fort on Sullivan's Island – an ideal place to set up Charleston's defense. He and his men began cutting down palmetto trees on the mainland and other nearby sea islands, and floating them back to Sullivan's Island. They worked day and night on building their simple square-shaped fort, driving upright palmetto logs into the ground and packing the walls with sand. On June 1, 1776, they had constructed only three-quarters of the fort before 50 English ships anchored just in front of the island. Many men doubted that Moultrie's fort could hold the powerful English ships at bay, and they sent their families away to hide in the countryside outside Charleston.

Outnumbered, outgunned, and seemingly not well protected, Moultrie's men vowed to stay and defend their city and their liberty. On June 28th, the battle began – the British fired cannons and guns at the little fort for nearly 12 hours and the Americans managed to hold them off with their limited supply of arms. To most everyone's surprise, the palmetto-tree fort stood up to English fire extremely well – the logs were so spongy that the cannonballs hurled at them just bounced right off!

By June 29th, many of the English ships were badly damaged and the fleet was forced to retreat. Just a few days later, the Declaration of Independence was signed. The courageous Charlestonians and their little palmetto-tree fort – later renamed for William Moultrie – had secured a victory that eventually helped America win the war for independence.

THE SWAMP FOX

In late 18th century warfare, two armies stood on either side of a battlefield, and when a signal was fired they ran at each other waving swords, bayonets, and guns. But during the American Revolution, Francis Marion, who was captain of South Carolina's militia, had a different idea. In 1780, he organized a small group of untrained and poorly-armed common men and trained them to stage surprise attacks that would catch the British unawares.

During these attacks, Marion and his men success-
fully sabotaged enemy communications and supply
lines, and even freed American prisoners.
They then disappeared to their hideout in
South Carolina's maze-like swamps,
where the English could not find them.
The English were so frustrated by Francis
Marion and his tactics that they nicknamed him
the "swamp fox", because he was unpredictable, sly,
and impossible to catch.

THE LITTLE BOAT
THAT COULD

Did you know that submarines were used during the American Civil War?
In fact, South Carolina was the site of the first successful submarine mission
in America, when the Confederate (Southern) boat *H.L. Hunley* was
launched on February 17, 1864. It was a night assault, and the small submarine set out from Charleston Harbor to attack the Federal ship *U.S.S.
Housatonic*. Eight men powered the boat using a back-breaking hand crank,
while one man steered and controlled the ship's depth. As they neared the
Housatonic, someone on deck spotted the vessel, but mistook it for a por-
poise. Minutes later, the *Hunley* fired a torpedo and the *Housatonic* went
down. But the explosion in the Union ship's hull also damaged the
Confederate sub, and caused it to sink as well. The historic submarine was
lost undersea until August 2000, when it was finally brought up to the sur-
face by marine archaeologists.

SOUTHERN HORSE-PITALITY

A horse is not allowed to enter the town of Fountain Inn unless he or she is
wearing pants.

Capital: Concord

State Flower: Purple Lilac

State Tree: White Birch

State Bird: Purple Finch

Land Area: 8,969 sq. mi.

New Hampshire pictures the natural rock formation nicknamed "The Old Man of the Mountain" on its quarter.

Rank in Size (Land Area): 44th

State Song: "Old New Hampshire"

Largest City: Manchester

Statehood Date: June 21, 1788

Nickname: Granite State

New Hampshire was named by Captain John Mason for the county of Hampshire in southern England.

NEW HAMPSHIRE: LIVE FREE OR DIE

When English Captain John Mason first laid eyes on New Hampshire in 1623, he was so taken with the land's beauty that he named the colony after his hometown of Hampshire. Considering some of the state's nicknames, it is easy to see what Mason found appealing. New Hampshire is mountainous and very green, and is often called "The Mother of Rivers" because five of New England's major rivers begin in the state: the Connecticut, the Merrimack, the Piscataqua, and Maine's Androscoggin and Saco Rivers. In all, New Hampshire has 40,000 miles of rivers and streams, not to mention nearly 1,500 lakes, ponds, and swimming holes.

New Hampshire's official nickname is "The Granite State," as granite mining was at one time a big industry in the state and continues to this day. Much of the granite in New Hampshire is located in its famous White Mountains (that appear white when the sun glares off the granite), which explains "The White Mountain State" nickname. The White Mountains are home to the Presidential Range, named after some of the early United States presidents. Because these mountains are often snowy, and always beautiful, the state has also earned the nickname "Switzerland of America."

A GRAND OLD MAN

The back of the New Hampshire quarter displays an unusual image – the pro-file of a man's face in stone. This distinguished face that sits on Mount Cannon in the Franconia Notch region is lovingly called the "Old Man of the Mountain." Beside the rocky profile on the quarter are the words "Live Free or Die," New Hampshire's state motto. There is also a crescent of nine stars, representing New Hampshire's role as the ninth state to enter the Union and ratify the U.S. Constitution.

The Old Man of the Mountain – often referred to by New Hampshire natives as "The Great Stone Face," "The Profile," and "The Old Man" – is an impor-tant emblem of the state's natural history. Believe it or not, the face was not the work of a sculptor, but was carved by Mother Nature herself. A long, long time ago, toward the end of the Ice Age, New Hampshire was completely buried under a glacier (a gigantic layer of ice). As Earth's climate grew warmer over thousands of years, the glacier shifted, shaping the rocks that lie beneath it. The moving glacier cut nooks and crannies into New Hampshire's White Mountain range, and the old man's profile appeared.

Although it looks like the Old Man's face is carved from one big block of gran-ite, it is actually comprised of five separate ledges that are stacked on top of one another. Two of the ledges form the forehead, one ledge forms the nose and one the lips, and another rounds out the chin. Together they create the illusion of a majestic profile.

New Hampshire is very proud of its natural wonder, and many tourists pause to admire it while vacationing in the beautiful forests and mountains of the state. The Old Man's imposing profile is also a symbol of the state's strength, and as famous New Hampshire native Daniel Webster stated, is "inspirational as to the kind of men the sons of the Granite State should be."

A MIGHTY MOUNTAIN

New Hampshire's most majestic mountain is the famous Mount Washington. The tip of Mount Washington rises an amazing 6,288 feet above sea level, making it the highest point in New Hampshire and all of New England. The weather in winter is very harsh, and temperatures often fall to 30 degrees below zero. In fact, it was at Mount Washington that the strongest wind on earth was recorded. On April 12, 1934, a storm whipped up the wind to an astonishing 231 miles per hour; that's stronger than hurricane-force winds, and about 20 times stronger than what we normally feel on a "windy" day!

NEW HAMPSHIRE AND BEYOND!

The first American ever to travel in space was Alan Shepard, born in East Derry on November 18, 1923. Shepard was sent into space on May 5, 1961, in a capsule that traveled 115 miles above the earth and orbited around it. Incredibly, the trip only took 15 minutes, about the time it takes most of us to eat breakfast! Shepard went on another mission in 1971, when he spent 10 days aboard the Apollo 14 space shuttle, and made the first landing in the moon's highlands.

Another New Hampshire native, Concord schoolteacher Christa McAuliffe, was chosen by NASA in 1986 to be the first civilian (or regular citizen) in space. Unfortunately, there was a problem with her spacecraft, the Challenger, and it exploded just seconds after lift-off, killing everyone aboard. New Hampshire honored McAuliffe's space attempt, and her achievements here on Earth, when it opened the Christa McAuliffe Planetarium in Concord in 1990.

THE PRIMARY PRIMARY

New Hampshire is home to a very important political process, the first presidential primary. During a primary, members of a political party meet to decide which of their nominees (party members who have been chosen to run for office) will continue the campaign, this time running against opponents from other parties. The New Hampshire Primary has helped to determine who will run for president since 1920.

THE LUNCH STATE

There are towns in New Hampshire named Sandwich and Rye.
Hungry, anyone?

Capital: Richmond

State Flower: American Dogwood

State Tree: American Dogwood

State Bird: Cardinal

Land Area: 39,598 sq. mi.

Rank in Size (Land Area): 37th

State Song: "Carry Me Back to Old Virginia"

Largest City: Virginia Beach

Statehood Date: June 25,1788

Nickname: Old Dominion State

Virginia is named for England's "Virgin Queen," Elizabeth I.

The settlement of Jamestown is celebrated on the Virginia coin.

VIRGINIA: THUS ALWAYS TO TYRANTS

In the late 16th century, Queen Elizabeth of England sent her friends Sir Walter Raleigh and Sir Humphrey Gilbert to explore America. When they reached the shores of the New World, they staked out an area and named it Virginia, in honor of their virgin queen.

In the 1660s, Virginia was one of England's most loyal colonies, and provided its motherland with much wealth. King Charles II favored Virginia so much that he added the colony's coat of arms to his royal shield, making it his 5th dominion (along with England, Ireland, Scotland, and France). From that time on, Virginia has been affectionately called "The Old Dominion State."

Another Virginia nickname comes from its role as the first English settlement in America. As the founder of the colonies, Virginia is often called "The Mother State." Both North Carolina and Maryland were carved out of the colony's land, so in a sense Virginia "gave birth" to these states as well.

Not only have states emerged from Virginia's soil, but it has also been the birthplace of four of our first five presidents – George Washington, Thomas Jefferson, James Madison, and James Monroe – lending it the name "The Mother of Presidents." As the state's various nicknames suggest, Virginia's contributions to the nation are varied and vast.

THREE TALL SHIPS

On the back of the Virginia quarter you will see three tall ships, the *Susan Constant*, *Godspeed*, and *Discovery*. These ships brought the first English settlers to America, anchoring in a place they named Jamestown. The word "quadricentennial" appears underneath the ships, because the quarter design commemorates Jamestown's 400th birthday in 2007.

In fact, Virginia was the first tract of American land to be chartered by King James I of England, in 1606, and Jamestown was the first colony. The King was eager to build a community in the New World, and urged his people to settle there. On December 20, 1606, the three small English ships set sail for America. When the colonists arrived, they sailed up the James River and built a little town along its banks. They built small cottages with thatched roofs and wooden clay-covered walls, and began to clear the land for farming.

Unfortunately, it was not long before hard times struck – since the ships had passed through other lands before they arrived in the New World, the passengers had picked up new diseases. During that first summer, many settlers died of these diseases because their bodies did not have defenses against them. Many of the Native Americans they met died, too. By fall, they had nearly run out of food, since many had been too busy looking for gold to farm the land. To make matters worse, relations between the settlers and the Native Americans were tense, and the occasional violence between them took its toll.

But by 1610, Lord De La Warr, the new Virginia governor, had arrived, and he started to set things straight. In 1613, a Virginian named John Rolfe married a woman named Pocahontas, the daughter of Native American Chief Powhatan. Their union soothed the conflict between the settlers and Native inhabitants, at least for a little while. It was during this peaceful time, nearly 400 years ago, that the Jamestown settlement, and its great Virginia colony, finally began to prosper.

A SPECIAL CEMETERY

One of America's most important landmarks, Arlington National Cemetery, is on the grounds of what was originally the home of President George Washington's adopted son, George Washington Parke Custis. General Robert E. Lee (the commander of the Confederate Army during the Civil War) later inherited the land when he married Custis's daughter. When Lee left his home for the battlefield, the house and grounds were taken over by Union soldiers, who set up camp there. By the Civil War's end, the United States had claimed the land and established a cemetery on the grounds. Over the years, some of America's most important figures have been buried there. Arlington National Cemetery is a monument to many historic Americans, and its most memorable site – the Tomb of the Unknown Soldier – stands as a memorial to all those who gave their lives for our country.

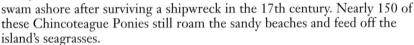

ALL THE PRETTY HORSES

Legend has it that the herd of horses living on Assateague Island, just off the Virginia coast, are the descendants of horses who swam ashore after surviving a shipwreck in the 17th century. Nearly 150 of these Chincoteague Ponies still roam the sandy beaches and feed off the island's seagrasses.

OF MONUMENTS AND MEN

The long, majestic Monument Avenue in Richmond is a memorial to the South's Civil War heroes. In 1906, the first statue, of Robert E. Lee on a horse, was placed at the head of Monument Avenue, facing South. People have interpreted Lee's position to mean that he is turning his back on his opponents to the North, and watching over his home in the South. The J.E.B. Stuart and Jefferson Davis statues on either side of Lee are also on horseback, and are considered symbols of the South's heroism and gentlemanly nature. The next statue, of "Stonewall" Jackson, faces north, as if he is forever acting as a protective stone wall against aggression. And finally, the position of Matthew Fontaine Maury's statue is viewed as an expression of peace. When considered as a whole, the images of war and peace on Monument Avenue create a lasting picture of the Civil War from a Confederate point of view.

TOSS AND BE TOSSED!

It is illegal to flip a coin in a Richmond eating establishment to decide who buys a cup of coffee.

PROGRAM

Founded by an act of Congress on April 2, 1792, the United States Mint has been operating for more than 200 years. The Mint produces between 14 and 20 billion circulating coins annually, as well as gold, silver, and platinum coins, proof coins and medals.

The first Mint was constructed in Philadelphia, Pennsylvania. Coins have been produced at this location since 1793. Since this was our only mint for many years, no mint mark was used until 1979 (except on 1942-1945 nickels). Still today the absence of a mint mark designates a coin as a product of the Philadelphia Mint, although a few coins including the quarters of the 50 State Quarters™ Program series do include a "P" mint mark. All engraving for U.S. coins is done at the Philadelphia Mint.

The Philadelphia Mint was our only mint until 1838 when the Dahlonega, Georgia (gold coins only), Charlotte, North Carolina (gold coins only), and New Orleans, Louisiana, mints were established. Later, the Carson City, Denver, San Francisco, and West Point mints were created.

For more information about the U.S. Mint, visit www.USMINT.gov.